THE DECLARATION OF INDEPENDENCE AND
ROBERT LIVINGSTON
OF NEW YORK

KATHY FURGANG

The Rosen Publishing Group's
PowerKids Press™
New York

For Leigh

Published in 2002 by The Rosen Publishing Group, Inc.
29 East 21st Street, New York, NY 10010

First Edition

Book design: Maria E. Melendez
Project Editor: Emily Raabe

Photo credits: Cover and title page, Portrait of Robert Livingston, map of the United States, and the Declaration of Independence document, p. 4 (portrait of Robert Livingston), p. 7 (ladies and gentlemen having tea, 1700s), p. 8 (New York City: Brooklyn Ferry, 1700s), p. 12 (Old State House, Philadelphia, 1700s) © North Wind Pictures; p. 15 (Declaration of Independence is written), p. 16 (signing the Declaration of Independence) © SuperStock; p. 11 (the burning of New York City during the night of 19 September 1776), p. 19 (the inauguration of George Washington as the first President at Federal Hall, New York, April 30, 1789) © The Granger Collection; p. 20 (painting of the Louisiana Purchase) © Bettmann/CORBIS.

Furgang, Kathy.
    The Declaration of Independence and Robert R. Livingston of New York / Kathy Furgang. — 1st ed.
        p. cm. — (Framers of the Declaration of Independence)
Includes index.
    ISBN 0-8239-5592-3
    1. Livingston, Robert R., 1746–1813—Juvenile literature. 2. United States. Declaration of Independence—Signers—Biography—Juvenile literature. 3. Statesmen—United States—Biography—Juvenile literature. 4. United States—Politics and government—To 1775—Juvenile literature. 5. United States—Politics and government—1775-–1783—Juvenile literature. 6. New York (N.Y.)—History—Colonial period, ca. 1600–1775—Juvenile literature. 7. New York (N.Y.)—History—Revolution, 1775–1783—Juvenile literature.
[1. Livingston, Robert R., 1746–1813. 2. United States. Declaration of Independence—Signers. 3. United States—Politics and government—1775–1783.] I. Title.
    E221 .F945 2002
    973.3'13'092—dc21   00-011920

Manufactured in the United States of America

CONTENTS

This is Robert as a young man. Robert's family owned a lot of land in New York City. They also owned a lot of the land north of the city, along the Hudson River.

YOUNG ROBERT LIVINGSTON

Robert R. Livingston was born on November 27, 1746, in New York City. Robert's father, also named Robert, was a well-known judge in the **colony** of New York.

Robert went to school at Kings College, which is now called Columbia University. Robert became a lawyer in 1770. He opened a law office with a friend named John Jay. Both men became famous. Robert helped to form the United States of America. His friend John became the most powerful judge in the new country.

COLONIAL LIFE

In the early 1700s, when Robert was growing up, the United States of America did not yet exist. America was made up of colonies that were ruled by the King of England. A lot of people in the colonies wanted freedom from England. People who wanted freedom were called **patriots**. Some people in the colonies thought that having a king was good for the colonies. They hoped that the colonies could make peace with the king. These people were called **loyalists**.

These colonists are wearing clothes made in the English style. They also are drinking tea, a custom brought from England.

This is New York City and the Hudson River in the 1700s. During the 1700s, boats brought goods from England up the Hudson River to New York City.

LIFE IN NEW YORK CITY

Although the earliest settlers in New York were Dutch, by the 1700s, many New York settlers were British. A lot of these New Yorkers felt that it would be best to keep peace with England. Both Robert and his father, however, were well-known patriots. In 1771, Robert lost his job as a judge because he spoke against the British government.

On April 19, 1775, in the town of Lexington, Massachusetts, patriots and British soldiers fired on one another. This battle began the **American Revolution**.

WAR IN THE COLONIES

Because New York City was an island, British soldiers were able to attack the city on all sides by boat. George Washington's Colonial Army tried to defend the city but could not hold out against the British troops. The British took over New York City for seven long years as the war raged. They made New York City their headquarters during the war. Many New Yorkers took their families to the nearby countryside so that they would be safe. The Livingston family lost some of their land in New York City during the war.

During the American Revolution, British soldiers set fires in New York City. Beautiful mansions were turned into army headquarters. The buildings were not cared for and they began to fall apart.

This is the Old State House in Philadelphia, Pennsylvania, where the representatives gathered during the Second Continental Congress.

ROBERT GIVES HIS OPINION

Soon after the war began, leaders from the different colonies met in Philadelphia to talk about the war. Another word for a political gathering is a congress. This gathering was the second time that the men met to discuss the war, so it was called the Second Continental Congress. Robert was at the Congress, **representing** the colony of New York. He was only 29 years old.

The representatives at the Second Continental Congress decided that they should be free from England's rule forever.

WHAT IS INDEPENDENCE?

The representatives at the Second Continental Congress decided to write a paper, known as a declaration, that would declare the new country's independence. To the representatives, independence meant that people should be treated equally. The representatives decided that the new country would not even have a king! Writing the declaration was a brave thing to do. If the British captured any of the men who signed the declaration, the men could be hanged as traitors to England.

The men who worked on the declaration were (left to right), Benjamin Franklin, Thomas Jefferson, John Adams, Robert Livingston, and Roger Sherman.

This shows the signing of the Declaration of Independence. The Declaration was copied and carried on horseback all over the new country so that all of the colonists could read it themselves.

THE DECLARATION OF INDEPENDENCE

Thomas Jefferson of Virginia wrote the **Declaration of Independence** with the help of Robert and three other men. The men presented the Declaration to the rest of the Congress on July 4, 1776. Not every member of Congress signed the Declaration. Some of them disagreed with parts of it. Robert himself did not sign the Declaration, but only because he was away in New York on July 4. The Declaration was approved by all of the representatives, however. A new country was born.

CAPITAL CITY

In 1783, the American Revolutionary War finally came to an end. America was free! New York City became the capital of the new United States of America. It was in a good location for the capital of the new country, halfway between the northern and the southern colonies. Robert was the **chancellor** of New York City. Only two presidents lived in New York City. In 1790 the capital was moved to Philadelphia for ten years. It was then moved to Washington, D.C., where it is today.

This shows Robert swearing in George Washington on the balcony of Federal Hall in New York City. After the ceremony Robert cried out, "Long live George Washington, president of the United States!"

This is an artist's painting of the Louisiana Purchase. The agreement also included parts of Colorado, Kansas, Louisiana, Montana, and Wyoming.

AFTER THE WAR

After the American Revolution ended, Robert helped to shape the new state of New York. When Robert was 35 years old, he became a **diplomat**, traveling to other countries to represent America. The greatest thing Robert did as a diplomat was to work out the **Louisiana Purchase** in 1803. This was a deal made between the United States and France. The United States bought land from France that became Arkansas, Iowa, Minnesota, Missouri, Nebraska, North Dakota, Oklahoma, and South Dakota.

LIFE ON HIS OWN

In 1804, Robert decided to work with a man named Robert Fulton on a new invention, the steamboat. The steamboat could travel much faster than the sailboats that people used to carry goods downriver. The steamboat was a great success. For many years, Robert Fulton and Robert Livingston controlled all of the steam traffic on the Hudson River.

Robert Livingston died on February 26, 1813, at his home in Clermont, New York. He was 67 years old.

GLOSSARY

American Revolution (uh-MER-uh-ken reh-vuh-LOO-shun) Battles that soldiers from the American colonies fought against England for freedom.

chancellor (CHAN-sell-er) A leader of a group or state.

colony (KAH-luh-nee) A place that is ruled by another country.

Declaration of Independence (deh-kluh-RAY-shun UV in-duh-PEN-dints) A paper signed on July 4, 1776, declaring that the American colonies were independent of England.

diplomat (DIH-ploh-maht) A representative of a country.

Louisiana Purchase (loo-ee-zee-AH-na PUHR-chaz) A deal made in 1803 between France and America that extended the borders of the United States.

loyalists (LOY-uh-listz) People who are loyal to a certain political party, government, or ruler.

patriots (PAY-tree-otz) People who love and defend their country.

representing (reh-prih-ZENT-ing) A person who is speaking or acting for a group.

INDEX

WEB SITES

To learn more about Robert R. Livingston and the Declaration of Independence, check out these Web sites:

http://www.aoc.gov/art/nshpages/livingst.htm

http://www.law.emory.edu/FEDERAL/conpict.html#indep